Strange Religion

Strange Religion

Jasmine Griffin

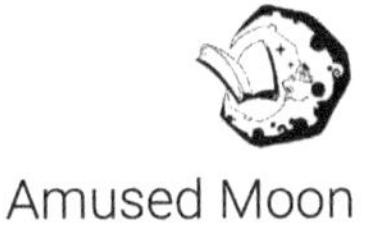

Amused Moon

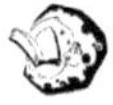

Library of Congress Control Number: 2024912150
ISBN 979-8-9869156-8-5
Subject Poetry Chapbook

Cover art design by author
Printed on acid free paper

First Printing, July 2024 Amused Moon
United States of America

CONTENTS

CONTENTS

CONTENTS

These poems were written in a dark space and time, when I was in the trenches of grief, struggling with mental illness, second guessing my faith, and in a period of self-discovery. While in a much better place, I still work on self-acceptance. My hope is that by putting these poems out in the world that they will resonate with even one person and make them feel a little less alone. Wherever faith is found, these words are for those in the Queer community still struggling with belief. For those with mental illness and for those dealing with loss. For those still choking on words left unsaid. For those who have been made to make themselves smaller. For those who find it hard to believe that there is a time when their struggles and suffering will come to an end. For those who feel as if there is no beauty to be found in their journey. You matter. You are important. You are accepted. You are loved. Use your voice. Take up space. You are beautifully and wonderfully made.

Fuck anyone who says differently.

DEDICATION

This chapbook is dedicated to anyone who has ever loved and accepted me for exactly who I am and anyone who has encouraged me to use and share my voice. Thank you, your support has meant more to me than you know.

This chapbook contains poems that have appeared in *Genre: Urban Arts* and *Cleaning Up Glitter*.

Special thanks to my family for their ongoing love and support. Huge thanks to all my writing friends and family in Cincinnati, Denver, and Pennsylvania. I wouldn't be the same without any of you and neither would my work. I love you all!

BOOK I: DECEPTION

The Process of Worship

Published in Genre: Urban Arts

I shouldn't have to give myself to you,

and yet, here I am,

shrinking myself down to microscopic level in the face of your desires.

Here I am,

building an altar dedicated to your image,

using my hair to wash your feet,

kneeling and praying five times a day in the direction that you said that your love came from,

but I haven't felt it yet.

Clutching my homemade rosary,

each bead representing the days that I've known you,

until my palms turned red and ached.

Rubbing your ego for good luck,

and wearing my Sunday best to your sermon about my inadequacies.

All while, preaching to the world that you can walk on water,

when you can't even swim.

Keeping my eyes downcast,

when giving you praise.

Hanging myself on the cross as sacrifice...

for *your* sins.

Resurrecting myself from my tomb when you need to use my body as a confessional again.

Cutting off my flesh for your nourishment.

Spilling my blood to quench your thirst.

Writing hymns about your body, your lips, and your touch.

As if,

you are a thing deserving homage.

As if, you are a thing deserving of praise.

Almighty in the highest,

As a god you are cruel,

Brutal,

Violent,

You are merciless,

A tyrant.

Demanding and I give.

I throw myself on your altar for you to take and take and take.

When there is nothing left of me where will you go to be fed?

That scares me more than anything,

Someone else,

more devout than I,

with more to give shouting out your name.

So, I kneel and wash your feet with my hair until the fear goes away.

Until I am blessed, with the smile you send down in my direction.

You should not be my religion.

And yet,

here I am.

Forgiveness

I am not God

I could forgive you

If I were

Serpent in Bloom

Serpents don't dwell in the dark,

Not in the mud they sling,

Not under the light of the blood moon.

Their venom can't find the vein,

They can't attract their prey,

If they slither away from the sun.

They linger amid blooms,

in vibrance,

Coiling around trees and hidden in petals,

Where their scales can reflect the beauty around them and entice.

Where they wrap their cool bodies around an unsuspecting hand,

searching to touch something fragile,

something precious.

Where they can press their icy scales against wounds and pretend to soothe the burn of their bites.

Fangs open as petals bloom,

Nectar sweet and venom acid,

A contrast there to captivate and mesmerize,

Bleed into the body and deteriorate the mind.

The last thing you see before you wilt is color,

Red, yellow, orange, and blue,

Psychedelic and swirling,

A parting gift, and ending fantasy,

The only apology for the deception.

BOOK II: IDENTITY

The Garden

I realized I was nude today, naked before the world.

The serpent told me,

After the apple touched my lips and I found it had already rotted.

I had gone mad long before the slinking sly thing had slithered at my feet.

It made me vulnerable I think, an easy target for the legless beast.

The madness.

That blessed garden was a guise for the truth.

I had been blissfully ignorant before the snake came.

With the serpent came insanity, a great monstrous thing slipping around my brain and making things unruly and unkempt.

Clear thoughts,

giving way to darkness.

Dark desires,

giving birth to unwanted truths.

I was tangled.

Muddled.

Confused.

Was it Adam or Lilith that had been created for me?

Who was meant to lay with me in that beautiful garden, a tangle of naked limbs and hair and breath and earth?

Who was the forbidden fruit?

Was I to be subservient or claim the rib and the trees and the fruit and whatever else I could take?

Should I be happy in this paradise?

"You should be," the snake hissed, "but you aren't. You will never be.

So, eat and accept the darkness."

It was right of course.

Misery,

was recognizable to my muddled mind.

Peace,

was the knowledge that the tree of good and evil kept from me.

So, I ate. The rotting fruit tasted familiar on my tongue; it was as comforting as it was wretched.

When I was cast out,

I welcomed it.

Of the World

I tried not to shut the world out,

fought the instinct tooth and nail.

Held the door between me and it open,

until I was no longer strong enough to do so.

It got even harder when I couldn't remember why I wanted to be part of it.

When making a list of pros and cons, my manic mind favored cons.

So, slowly but surely the shutting down commenced,

and I began to just go through the motions.

When going through my daily routine I kept asking myself,

"Does this seem normal?"

"Can they tell, that it's for show?"

"Can they tell, that I'm not okay?"

But it's hard to perceive how the world perceives you,

                especially when you're no longer connected to it.

So how did I get back?

 I'm not always sure that I am.

   Maybe I trust myself more or maybe I stopped trusting other people less.

   Maybe I felt so isolated and alone,

   that I couldn't help but open the door back up.

Because even if a connection isn't always wanted,

                it's needed.

Atonement for the Self

Published in *Cleaning Up Glitter*

I am exhausted,

from creating a world.

A world that protects me from the world I know.

A world that tells me it's okay to love who I love and to hate myself in equal measure.

One of splendor and shame,

where everything that isn't of the norm remains unspoken,

and so....

there is silence.

Blissful and broken silence that gives no voice to the images in my head.

A world that shows me how I'm going to die,

(more than likely by my own hands),

and one that shows me how I want to live,

(free and by my own rules).

A world of weakness,

where I speak softly for fear of being heard.

And of light,

where I shine so brightly it can almost reach the service through the mud of negativity and the nightmares of failure.

Of hope,

that has me on my hands and knees praying for the will to survive,
and depression,

that keeps me in bed for days and has my apartment so cluttered that I may not see the floor for weeks.

One that is ugly and thriving and mine.

I did not rest on the seventh day,

 though my eyes were heavy,

and my body was limp.

 I did not rest.

There was too much to atone for.

I locked myself up in a closet to pray.

 Sprinkled rice on the ground,

and knelt down on my knees.

                    Clasped my hands and bowed my head.

Murmured confessions softly as a lullaby,

of all the things I dared not shout.

Ignored the serpent at my feet that whispered, "Even the most devout can be broken."

                                        I knew that already.

I was that.

Shattered beyond repair.

I prayed in screams and in whispers.

The prayers I needed to be heard much more than things long kept secret.

I prayed the rosary three times.

Then once more for good measure.

I'm not Catholic, just wanted to cover my bases.

As I said before there was much to atone for.

I wore only white,

hoping it when make me pure,

though my skin was too dark for the world to believe it so.

Cursed the blood on my hands when it wouldn't wash out.

Where had it come from?

The cuts on my wrist that had long since healed?

Had the scars that once stripped my skin reawakened?

Had the wounds reopened when the feelings that caused them refused to go away?

I killed my true self,

hid the body under the label that society had given me.

Buried it six feet under,

and then stomped it down two more feet for good measure.

It was better that way,

or so I was told.

Mustn't stray from the expected.

Must be the Mammy,

the daughter,

so strong and unfeeling.

Must take the pain with my head held high.

Be the mule of the world like all my other black sisters!

I don't need no man but God!

Don't need no woman but Mary but not Magdalene. Never Magdalene (oh but her kisses are so sweet)!

Out, damned spot! Wash until the hands are red and raw and the thoughts go back to the shadows where they belong.

I am a virgin.

But I am not Mary.

Too dark for that.

Not pious enough.

The only things conceived in me, immaculate or otherwise, are rage, depression and anxiety.

Can this darkness be my savior?

Can I be baptized in screams that only reach my own ears without drowning?

Can the worry that steals my sleep, die for my sins?

There's nothing virtuous here.

Sorry to disappoint.

I am no saint.

I am my own maker and what monster have I created?

I whipped myself in penance,

a lash for each time I had desired a man.

Three for each time I had desired another woman.

Six for each time I had spoken out of turn.

Nine for each time my eyes remained open when others would have them be closed.

After a while I stopped counting.

I bled but I did not feel.

Oh, but I *wanted* to feel.

Wouldn't it be grand to know what feeling was,

even if it was an ache so raw it tore me up from the inside.

But as a black woman I am immune to pain.

At least that's what they tell me.

I am a strong black woman who don't need no man.

No woman but Mary! Never Magdalene (no matter how soft her skin)!

No man but God! Hallelujah! Let the church say Amen!

As I laid to rest,

the world I had spent so much time creating,

my prayers finally stopped.

Had they been ignored?

Or have they been answered?

By me?

By God?

My world is not dead or lost, just open. Bleeding out despite my best efforts. Leaking out into the real world.

When had I stopped being afraid? (I had not, not really).

My truth risen from the grave. (Still trying to surface that last two feet).

When had I been gifted the blessing of exploration?

The blood finally washed clean. (Hands rubbed raw, but I finally felt the ache).

When will my deliverance come?

Forgive me Father for I have sinned.

Am I wrong to want to be at rest?

Forgive me Father, for I have sinned.

I am your child, and I am what you created.

Forgive me, Father. For I have sinned.

The Definition of Self

Who am I?

There's the question of the ages.

There are labels I fit under,

I suppose.

Though,

that depends on whose definition you use.

If it's not my own,

then the perspective gets skewed into something unfitting.

So, who am I?

Black is one part,

female another.

However, to many people certain aspects of my femininity
would be found wanting.

Hell, certain aspects of my blackness too.

Maybe the definition is in the sex,

or lack thereof.

Am I lonely? Yes.

Straight? Nope.

Gay? Not quite.

Depends on who they are,

or who I am,

Or the moment.

So, who am I, really?

An artist? I'd like to think so.

You are one if you create things, be them ugly or beautiful.

You create art when you create the truth, your truth.

So, who am I, truly?

Who the fuck knows?

I change so much minute to minute,

thought to thought,

and experience to experience.

Is the self really something to be defined?

Or should it just be accepted?

Embraced, every minute,

every hour,

and every second.

But how can you embrace what has no definition?

What boggles the mind and has no real limits.

That's, perhaps, the real question.

I guess the answer would be with open arms,

And an open mind.

With the love that the outside world denies it,

And the care that others refuse to show.

BOOK III: LOVE & GRIEF

Gently Flows the River

The water ripples as softly as your hand on my skin,
As your voice,
As your embrace.

The waves barely disturbed the surface,
Rising and falling in the same way that I fell for you,
In pieces,
In drops,
Not knowing that eventually it would build into a roaring tide.

But fear forbid me to speak the words,
Kept them trapped under the surface,
As I stood on the water's edge and watched them sink deeper.

I was afraid that you would be taken from me,
Gone as a quickly as a pebble skipping across the surface,
One skip,

Two jumps,
And lost under the water.

You were taken anyway,
In death,
And the words stayed choked in my throat even as I watched
you slip away,
The river stayed eerily still aside from the disturbance that my
tears caused as they dropped into the water one by one.

I knew that,
 any prayers for your resurrection would be in vain,
And so, I,
Whispered the words to the water,
The words I could never utter while you breathed air,
The sound echoing louder than the flow of it through the
rocks,
And I hoped that wherever you were,
 you could hear them.

Sleep

Since you died,

I haven't gotten much sleep.

I never realized how many times you got me out of my own head, until you weren't there to do it anymore.

When it first happened,

when I lost you,

I stayed awake and prayed God would take me too.

That is,

when I wasn't feeling guilty over not being taken instead.

That was in the beginning,

When it first hit me that you were really gone.

Now,

Other things keep me up at night.

The things I want to tell you about but can't.

Some people, compare death to sleep,

when in truth they are nothing alike.

Death has a sort of permanence that sleep does not.

I can wake up from a nightmare.

I can forget it and move on.

I can't forget you.

I can't wake up from this.

You can't wake up from death.

On the bad nights,

the truly bad nights,

the nights where my mind is not completely my own,

I think about digging up your grave and bringing you back from the dead like

Frankenstein's monster.

Would you be as eloquent?

Would you remember me?

Would you resent me for disturbing your peace because I could not find my own?

We would resent each other, I think.

You'd resent me for taking away your escape.

For taking you away from your family that died before you,

once again.

Your children.

Your sister.

Your mother.

You'd hate me for turning your death into sleep.

I'd hate you for taking my sleep in the first place.

For leaving me here alive with the mess that I am.

Without my best friend,

and only my cat and my word processor to talk to me about my worries and self-loathing in your place,

over Sleepy Time tea that doesn't fucking work.

We'd be monsters you and me and maybe you'd want me dead.

I wouldn't fight it,

I'd welcome it.

It'd be beautiful.

A tragic sort of irony,

to finally receive rest,

from the one who took my sleep from me.

Faith

I thought that my faith died with you,

With your smile,

With your laughter,

With the way that you coiled your hair around your fist before you tied it up,

With the drunken moment that you burst into the bathroom as I showered to scream how much you loved me,

With the feel of your head on my shoulder,

With the way that you offered me more forgiveness than I offered myself,

With the years of connections and separations,

With you moving on and me staying stagnant,

But always,

always you would answer when I called,

With the, deafening beep of hospital machines and final words
that you could not hear.

Then slowly,

so slowly,

I found faith in other things,

Felt remorse and guilt,

   even as my vitality was restored years after your heart stopped
beating.

But the first thing,

the very first thing,

that I found faith in after you left the world behind,

was the thought that your faith in me hadn't died with you,

I knew then,

   that I had to keep going.

BOOK IV:
RESTORATION

Paper Gods

Real gods demand blood,

lambs slaughtered on altars.

Crimson dripping over stone while words of devotion fall from lips.

Humans chained as tribute to monsters.

The gods of my dreams demand blood.

Blood staining keyboard keys,

burgundy droplets that are a bitch to get out.

Sweat dripping from my forehead,

as deadlines approach.

Tears falling from my eyes,

when the right words won't come,

and when they do,

and it's as hard to write them,

as it is to say them aloud.

Balled up paper.

Ink-stained fingers.

My gods are the gods of Baldwin, and Hurston, and Hughes.

Gods, whose church lies, in between pages. Where the pews are filled with readers and all the ministers preach through the pen.

To those gods I will confess my sins.

To those gods I'll bleed myself dry.

Promised Land

If I made it to the land of milk and honey,

> would there be as much judgement as there is here on Earth?

Could I live freely?

> Is it possible for someone like me?

Could I make the walls around me,

> crumble with my screams?

> Would the gates open if I knelt day and night?

If I slaughtered a lamb on the altar of my sins?

> If I made it to the land of milk and honey,

Would I find the hope you promised me?

Renewal

I've baptized myself in the words of those that came before me,

    made a bible of the lessons that came from their
experiences.

Embraced myself with invisible arms,

    and called it faith in the unknown.

Nothing is ever lost or forgotten,

    but it is reshaped and reformed as I have been,

again,

and *again*,

and AGAIN.

    Hopefully into something,

that is,

though misshapen,

though flawed,

though Queer,

though unstable....,

                                        still lovable,

                                          still beautiful,

                                          still learning,

                                          still seeking,

                                          still joyful,

                                          still ME.